The Lantern Cage

Kelly Grovier was born in Grand Rapids, Michigan, and educated at the University of California, Los Angeles, and Oxford University. He has written widely on the poetry of the eighteenth and nineteenth centuries and is co-founder of the scholarly journal *European Romantic Review*. He is a regular contributor to the *Times Literary Supplement* and author of the survey of contemporary art *100 Works of Art That Will Define Our Age* (Thames & Hudson). He currently lives in Ireland. This is his third collection of poems.

KELLY GROVIER

The Lantern Cage

Oxford*Poets*

CARCANET

First published in Great Britain in 2014 by
Carcanet Press Limited
Alliance House
Cross Street
Manchester M2 7AQ

www.carcanet.co.uk

A CIP catalogue record for this book is available from the British Library

ISBN 978 1 90618 813 9

The publisher acknowledges financial assistance from Arts Council England

Typeset by XL Publishing Services, Exmouth

for Sinéad

Acknowledgements

I am grateful to the editors of the following websites and publications, where versions of these poems appeared for the first time: *Doric* (Oliver Wood, 2012), *The Hippocrates Prize Anthology of Poetry*, *Oxford Poetry*, *PN Review*, *The Poetry Archive*, and *Tin Mal / Cut Ground* (Kerlin Gallery, Dublin).

Contents

I walk out of the dark and into the dark and sit down and wait.
— Charles Bukowski

Keeping time

It started by accident:
a chance pluck

        on the lip
of a stem-glass filling

with water. Soon,
I found the voice
        of all things

could be sharpened, shaped,
sculpted to the ear

        of a ghost,
like me. Before long, I was rosining

rain, tightening the pitch-
black of a butterfly's

scales, tuning
forks in the road. For a time,

the universe
        was harmonious,

strung like a wind-
        chime of bones,

shadows clicking
into place, everything, even the stars,

grooving to the skeleton
keys of the dead.

Strange Water

Scuffing the pebbled
unpeopled beach

how much of who we are
lies scattered

              among the ropes
of slippering kelp:

                  voices
in unlifted shells,

unreflected skies in the unreached
rockpools. Another world

is all around us,
              shifting

in undeciphered sands:
the scrawl

           of seagull shadows
and the waves' loosening

grammar, while at your feet
strange water
              is washing something

you'll either bend to
or ignore.

Sluice

in memory of Seamus Heaney

There is a lane, a country turn
of guelder rose and spindle

some part of me swerves to
every time I pass this way –

two wheel-wide lines
of gravelly crunch my living ghost

peels off to meet, tracking
the hedgerow down to a quiet

stream-bed I feel is there, rolls
his sleeve and plunges wrist-deep

in a babble of waterlight –
soul soused in a sluice of morning –

and, once back, scrabbles greedy
in the slosh (azurite and zinc,

pyrite and lead) finds himself
rich again, rich beyond words.

Rearview

Someone is having a dream
about the dark

variegated eyes of raccoons and elk
and a long

        perforated road
that runs between

the margins
of bodies – bodies of slumped

badgers and the bristle
of a crumpled fox;

and in the language
        of the dream,

these violent expirations
are recognised
        as words,

arranged
        by the receding

syntax of the rearview,
        only the story

they compose is one
of a ghostly
        breathing, of hooves

cocked in a gauze
of ficus and fir;
        it's one of bright

                    scratches of leaves
sparking the autumn

dusk, and in the distance,
                         growing

stronger through the fog,
a kind of punctuation,

                    whose object
is larger than it appears.

The Edge

Sitting here, watching the moon stream
and waiting for the stars to shuffle
their invisible tracks, all this winter evening needs

is a soundscape – notes to bind the soul
with strings, rhythm to carry it
to the very edge of itself. I think about that

as I struggle to remember what it was
the mystic Robert Fludd once said
about music being the only vestige

of our angelic state – melodies
suspended in the tar of mind like fossils
of a lost paradise. Suddenly, the sky changes discs

and I feel the ambient vibrations of something
jangling in the distance, moving closer,
gathering steady like the faint

knowledge of a place I've been to, mapped
inside me – an outskirt, whose ghostlit streets
I recognise, but have no name.

A Very Short Introduction to Hearing

Move closer, but be careful
not to disturb
         the balance –

the fragile equilibrium
that keeps
         the universe

from slipping. Lean in,
but never so tight

         as to jar the spirit
level of being. Even

the inward music
of a lifted shell,

         whose notes
are fitted to the mind's

ear, must first finesse
the dark

         vestibules of the osseous
labyrinth, its anvil

         and hammer,
must first transcend

a maze of nerve and muscle.

In a time before us, before
the inventions

         of silence, sound
was auxiliary to the technologies

of jaw, whose brute
fossils still

          line our temples. Now,
every syllable is a ghost, every word

an excavation –

          ancestral, prophetic.
Be here, but remember

that hereness
is merely an echo

          of something past
and coming – a double,

the reflection
          of a breathing that occurred
somewhere else,

long before,
          and long after.

King's Hall

It could hardly have been longer
than a second,

            staring sleepless
from the third-floor flat,

to catch sight of the old man's
measured stride,

            the swing
of his walking stick, scruff

of beard and wasted frame,
gliding along

            the water's edge
in the purple

half-light of a summer's 4 a.m. –
more like something dreamt

than living:
            a breathing

iridescence, an idea.
And I do not think

a week has passed
            in the intervening

years, my mind
            hasn't turned

to his curious reflex, his unfathered
eyes, the unmirrorable

motion of his amphibious gait,
hasn't read

        into the invisible
scrawl of his stroke,

           a meaning
deeper than the pocked sand,

wondered what smooth formula
freed the friction

         of sense
and skin, and looking up,

           reflected
for an instant

         whose groggy blink
may have millimetred me

           in a flash
of accidental grace:

the moon calculating posture,
physiques syncing

         to the ungainly
ocean, the uncoordinated rain.

Slide

From where I sit, I can see
the jetty's slow sloping stairs
easing into water, children

spooling crab lines, a fray of salt-
worn tether and the sodden
ghosts of a tide: six or seven

wave-warped steps on which,
from where I sit, you can see
the dead emerge at 3 a.m.

in their sodium-inflected wetsuits
and awkward gear. They too
hold hands as they web along

the prom, staring at the distant
line where day and night split
hairs; only the horizon for them

means something different,
like returning to a playground
years later to find the dimensions

changed, diminished: the space
between the swing and slide
growing smaller and smaller.

Button

Only because the moon hit it
square between the eyes

did I notice the small
opalescent button

half-hidden in the grass,
a few feet from our door.

Old-style: the kind
your grandmother fishes

special from a special box
for a special cardy she's knitting

for a special day – a christening,
or her favourite grandson's special

school performance.
I thought of the other

five or six she'd scrounged for,
still hanging

by a thread, and the sprig
of woollen fray

that finally let it go,
and couldn't help wondering

what it was that did it –
what sudden gesture

slipped it loose
to clatter and roll unnoticed

from her heart – reaching
for a locket she'd lost

years ago, or the slow sign
of a cross she made

without thinking,
one moonless evening,

a few feet from a stranger's door,
her crooked fingers trembling

as she stitched tight
the four corners of her soul.

Uncollected

Stepping from the humid
laureateship of my shower

and the head's steady
indiscriminate applause,

I wonder how many
poems have washed away

in there, etched in steam
on the steamless mirror –

only the fleeting punctuation
of a tissue's corner, dabbed

into place on the long-
suffering chin, proof

of their enduring
untranscribable genius.

Squint

A book borrowed, given, or taken away
  and the gap it leaves on the awkward shelf –
    some words stay back and some were never there;

like names you half-remember, squint to say,
  whose syllables swerve from the thing itself:
    you're never really here nor quite elsewhere.

The Last Line

You there, reading this – whose eyes are heirs
of mine and mine the ghost of yours –

whatever you do, don't look ahead or drop
your gaze to glance at how these lines

will end. Keep your concentration focused here,
somewhere in the middle, so that this,

our slow synchronised stare, will never dissolve
into the crossed tease of a finished poem,

so we can continue a little longer the mysterious
syntax of looking across time – so that I,

haunting the words you are reading now,
can still feel the invisible connection of two

people wondering over the same turn
of phrase, the same punch-line, that parting shot:

look up, wherever you are, you've always been.

Jackdaw

Out of the blue, night
drags its smudgy eraser
over chimneys and trees
and even a few sheep

unfinished in the field,
which, at the best of times,
are pretty fuzzy. Soon,
a hand will begin tidying

the edges, measuring things.
But for now, the world
is disappearance –
jackdaws and darkness

shaking each other's feathers;
senses giving way
to other senses, and words,
to the opposite of words.

Slip

A small slip of paper,
no larger than the page

you are holding in your hands,
is drifting down

                Oxford Street,
catching, every few steps,

the back of someone's heel
or stockinged calf,

                    before floating on
unnoticed by the crowd –

as though it were a leaf
that shed itself

                 from the book
of someone's life, sliding

through his fingers, to bring
its appalling news

                 to the next person
on its list: someone

who is just now
stepping out of a newsagent,

or exiting the Tube and bending down
to stop a scrap of litter,

                   finds herself
staring into a maze

of words that will alter things
forever,

   making it impossible
to return home

or to speak to her husband,
ever to see her children again

or visit her parents' graves,
something so huge

      it could only fit
on a small slip of paper,

no larger than the page
you are holding in your hands.

The Three Rs

The world always begins
with a phrase – instinctive,

unthinking – an utterance
from which meaning

follows only gradually, if ever,
conjugating itself in water, heat,

and the reactions trigger
further reactions: the angle

of one's heart, long divisions
of suffering. Somewhere,

a girl is holding a sign: the name
of a passenger whose train

will never arrive. Meanwhile
I am here, talking to you,

banging on about the effing
ineffable, never knowing

whether a stranger
in another world, waiting

on a platform, is ever going
to spell my name right.

What Happened

They were all reading, every one of them –
eyes pinned to pulp and tabloid, crossword

or obituary, glossed tat and the op–ed page.
Each oblivious to the ruck and judder

of the white-knuckled tracks as we joggled
to the edge. And this is worth recording,

I tell you, not for what it says
about the literate tug of random rails,

but to register what happened
when the carriage shuddered short,

jolting us from our private fictions –
the phrase and fragment frozen to each face

composed themselves into a calm – syntactical,
simultaneous – an eloquent blankness that hung

an instant in the air, then shattered
into accents, syllables, prayer.

The Art of Angling

for Jacky Klein

Snapping the covers shut,
my mind

       is suddenly the air
that gusts from deep inside

the spine, as though the book
has been holding its breath

for years. I can't help thinking
of all the other puffs,

             gasping
between the pages

on the antiquarian shelves,
and wonder what good

might come from flinging
through the aisles,

            cracking
the volumes open,

clapping them closed, one
by one, tipping

the crowded cases over –
the dank air fizzing

with dust, catching
the evening sunlight like salmon

in a late summer's stream.

The Goldbeater's Arm

In *A Tale of Two Cities*, Dickens tells
of 'a quiet street corner, not far

from Soho Square'
and 'a building at the back

where a plane-tree rustled
its green leaves' – a place where gold

is 'to be beaten
by some mysterious giant

who had a golden arm starting
out of the wall'. And this is worth

remembering, should you ever
find yourself

                pursued by footsteps
in the final seconds

of the world: that arm is still
there, still

            flexed in gilt
above the old Guild's door.

And should you barely make it
breathless to the low

                    stone step,
desperate for the ancient door

to swing open,
as a huge hammer looms

heavy above you,
think of the others – fifty,

a hundred yards back –
who came to Dickens a little too late,

missing it
by that much, and looking up,

will never see the roll
of its muscular sleeve, its forearm start

to straighten, the moon
of its flat head

             flash full,
as the last star's spark

sparks out.

Snakeskin

For some, the equation is tied
to the rhythm

              of snowdrops,
aconites, the slow dilation

of a winter's iris. For others,
the frequency

              is more erratic,
like the formulae

of sunsets, auroras of autumn,
skitters of fuchsia

across a snakeskin sky.
For me, the theorem remains

conjectural – the universe,
too mean

              a margin to prove
the ellipses of beauty,

tangents of tears, figures
whose invisible calculation

God keeps
under lough and quay.

I'll Have a Bite of Yours

So much talk these days of parallel worlds,
of string theories and quantum leaps –

of a universe layered with layers of universes.
But what could it mean, this endless wedding cake

of time and space – each of us invisibly
auditioning each others' lives, inches apart,

light years? Think of all the shoes. No wonder they come
in so many sizes. As if it were all a cosmic *ceilidh*:

bodies and souls half-cut, looping in a lace
of sloping arms. I imagine the infinite rehearsals of me,

and me infinitely rehearsing everyone else:
seven billion Kellys squared, spinning in galaxies flung

like caster sugar over rising wheels of fondant, radiused
with a knife gripped by trembling hands, slicing

through a chaos of centuries, stars, and you – eyes prismed
beautiful through eternity, their exponential blue

desperate to know if I am ever gonna share that thing.

Crossing

Tonight, the moon invites a sense
of crossing –

        not of movement
or journey or the slow conveyance

of bodies across a dark
expanse – not the linear equations

of a to b. As though, in the distance
of one's self,

        you see
something ascending a steep slope,

and with it comes talk
of an exchange, an acceptance.

Look at your hands.
What do you think they're for?

A Nose for Science

Bookless, bored, peering into a stranger's newspaper
on the crowded train, my eye catches on a story

about a team of scientists in Prague
digging for the remains of Tycho Brahe.

I squint in close to read
how they dragged skeletons from the nave of a church

in the Old Town Square, dusted the skulls
for a verdigris ghost haunting the bridge

between his sockets, looking for evidence
of the copper prosthetic he wore

for what was lost in a duel.
I wonder what they made of it, his bones,

when the stone floor burst open, spilling
with light. Did they think it had returned

after all these centuries, to bring news of strange scents
wafting from the skies – Hale-Bopps and blitzkrieg,

black holes, dark matter – a severed sniff forever
scrunching forward, inch by inch,

light-year after light-year, still sticking itself
where it doesn't belong?

Walking Stewart

I met him and shook hands with him under Somerset House… Thence I went by the very shortest road (i.e. through Moor Street, Soho – for I am learned in many quarters of London) towards a point which necessarily led me through Tottenham Court Road; I stopped nowhere, and walked fast; yet so it was that in Tottenham Court Road I was not overtaken by (that was comprehensible), but overtook Walking Stewart.

– Thomas De Quincey, 'Walking Stewart',
London Magazine, 1822

Striding through Soho, a stranger waiting
at the other end, no chance to pause

and put down the lines you are reading now,
I find myself thinking of Walking Stewart

who strolled these streets centuries ago,
and his belief that we are all anagrams of each other,

each an endless flux of atoms forever
rearranging themselves – now composing

the paragraph of you, now articulating the sentence
of me – none of us the same expression one moment

to the next. And I wonder how many molecules
that once enunciated Stewart are still swirling

this neighbourhood, as I kitty-corner up Moor Street,
heading west to Golden Square – wonder

what proportion of him I might meet, or even be,
when I arrive. Or perhaps I'll recognise him

straightaway – a semblance of myself, an alternate
spelling of a person I once was or will one day be –

like reading for the first time a poem whose words
you know you know by heart – its syllables scribbled

in your blood – though no one's ever stopped
to write them down.

The Angle

after Rilke

Given a choice between the sun
that rises from inside us,

or the sea that comes to life
like an old memory,

the gull will always pick the angle
of crust. For there is nothing

that we've been or must unlearn
that the waves haven't told us –

nothing that the dawn can hide
under its wrinkled skin. Pinch the sand

between your toes; the world is aching
to know if it's dreaming.

The Edwin Smith Papyrus

for Anthony Mosawi

When word came, we rugged the humps, grabbed our flasks,
    set off in pairs under an aching skull
of stars across the desert. There were risks,
    true, but not going was riskier still.

It took the parched throat of three days to reach
    the wind-shattered obelisks of Luxor –
its granite needle – and two more to touch
    the crumbling lips of the thing we'd come for:

an ancient weave of pith and soot-soaked wax –
    seventeen leaves of fragile hieroglyph
fixed in incense, ochre and gum to coax
    diseases from the body, dying from life.

These were the pharaoh's physician's secrets,
    we were assured, silent for centuries –
a lost calculus for adding spirits
    to salve, mapping the brain, suturing eyes.

We haggled hard for those illegible
    rags, then slid a purse across the table,
loped back beneath an incorrigible
    moon that turned our shadows to syllable.

Now, everything I am inflects the earth
    as atoms, pixels, ghosts on an X-ray –
a loosening helix of rhyme whose worth
    vibrates invisibly in the mind's eye.

Lines on a Da Vinci Skull

Drowsing the crowded exhibition,
our eyes scuff past still lives and statues,

a case of crumbling letters – fragments
and folios – until we reach a faint

pen-and-ink plotted for some abandoned
screed: a cranium sawn in two –

quoins and crevices shaded like sea caves –
and gridded across it all, a charcoal X

pies the chasm into quadrants, marking
a spot two inches behind the eyes. Here,

the inner and outer worlds pin-hole
to a mystical nub: *senso commune*; here,

imagined compasses pivot, their splayed limbs
squaring the empty circle, whales periscope

to the surface of being, and in the shifting
tangle of nib and pigment, a dusky girl

with deep mirroring eyes smiles incalculably
then erases herself, like a shadow over stone.

The Music Lesson

It comes down to the gentle curve,
not of the girl's neck,

                or slope
of shoulder, still tense

from what was whispered
beyond the vanishing

                point
of words, but of how our vision

bends through a plane
that angles time

the way water tempers
light, deflecting
                what we see
from what we can't

outside the askanced window:
the thinning shadows

of an afternoon, workmen
hauling shingles, or something

that has never before occurred
and never will again, bodied

in a strange heat, something unsuited
to a painting (let alone a poem) –

something that belongs forever
over there.

The Wanderer

after Mark Alexander's darkened version of Caspar David Friedrich's
Wanderer Above the Sea Fog

To say he stands for us, to feel our gaze
merging into his – seer and seen colliding
in the distance of his stare, beyond the fiction

of his brow – to insist he shares our stance,
back forever turning to the world, is to say nothing
of the slow dilation of his eyes, centuries wide,

their gradual incineration of air, to collude
in the myth of history's irreversible drag.
By my watch, it's late November 2011,

neutrinos are moving faster than they should,
and the artist still has time to return to easel and spirit,
still has time to blot us in or to blot us out.

Vertical Horizons

for Sean Scully

1. *Doric Light*

I begin to believe nothingness
will take different forms,
the way water knows itself
in the frost's blurring mirror,

remembers its hands
in forgetfulness of snow.
Here, emptiness gathers
to chisel and stone –

the hammered column
and the hammering rain;
and the soul assembles
the shapes it will need

after the afterlife: lintels
of dusklight, sills of moon.
Here, time smoothes
to cornice and eave, blank

pediments under which
we will emerge, the guiding
and the guided: a thing breathing
and the thing that breathed.

2. *Four Dark Mirrors*

In time, we come to see ourselves
as if from a distance of adjoining rooms –
a space hung with still unfolding
works: maps, perhaps, scraped clean

of latitude and parish – a misalignment of eyes:
the you staring and the you stared at.
In *Four Dark Mirrors*, the artist fixes us
in an endless deferral of reflection,

as though the surface has filled itself
with so much seeing, and what reverberates
back is not a ricochet of glance
across exterior space, not the coaxing

of selves in darkening glass,
but something merging from inside:
a reconciliation, the awkward meeting
of who you are and who you ought to be.

3. *Doric Brown*

Strange to hear one's soul ask itself
how much of you is still willing
to play along with the endless

switching on of the lights, the rinsing
of the cup. To catch it questioning
what part remains signed up to all this

chit-chat and *hoo-hah*. Every day is either
affirmation or decline. Even the sea
nods its head. In *Doric Brown*,

the yeses and nos divide
like angular amoebae; presence
elbows absence – something

from nothing, here nor there.
That's one way of seeing it. I prefer
to think the cards are being

shuffled again: a hand dealing
from the bottom of the deck.
Beware the Drowning Man

and the Two of Swords. Keep your eye
on the Poker-faced Moon.
No telling what's up his sleeve.

Rushlight

Somewhere, a girl is sitting in the dark
composing a history

                of illumination,
drawing her reader through a flicker

of cave to the vacuum
of filaments, tracing the arc

from tungsten to induction,
Aladdin to Argand. And she pauses

to reflect on the last to roll
a Victorian rushlight,

                  to pluck the stalk
and peel its greening rind, the last

to run his nail along the sponged pith
and steep it

          in the fat of a fulmar,
to smear the slickened vein

with beeswax, and she wonders
if he senses something fusing

in the final wick: shapes of a self
scraping the scullery wall,

brushing the frosted window – stars
scribbling in the distance –

                a way of seeing
that will never burn so sharp again.

Yellow Light Folding

for Liliane Tomasko

According to etymologists, 'text',
'texture' and 'textile' spring from the self-
same root: Latin 'textus' meaning 'style',
'tissue' – the Gospel truth. And sew,

you see, one weaves a tale, spins
yarns, loses the thread of thought
and plot. Take Liliane's lines of oil
on linen, *Yellow Light Folding*;

take its crumpled stitch on stitch,
its wrinkled metaphor of fabric cloaking
fabric. Here, what once was and still
might be are tugged tight as bodies,

or the memory of shapes whose absence
resists perspective, the way language
keeps its form long after meaning
has departed, leaving only traces

of feeling: a gauze of dusk
and shadow, blood and bone, a loom
of years in which we find ourselves
lost for words.

Orrery

for my mother

We come to you in the cold quiet
of the astronomer's cabinet –
a capsized spider spinning

polished spheres, wound
in a burr of whirling –
and my mind catches

on the tired, untuned teeth
of your gold and gaudy gears,
hurling headlong through heaven

invisible wires, fusing the darkness
to a jitter of stars.

On the Koi-ness of Time

Since it has come,
this moment,
finning to the surface

of a mooned lake,
we are responsible to it
and to every puzzled scale

in its lucent being.
Only through the weave
of its complicated skin

can we rise
to the balance
of our own breathing.

Since it has come,
this synchronicity of light
and air, we must

bend to it,
before the wrist twitches
and the line snaps.

The Last Almanac

for Jem Poster

They come to me in flashes, the astrologers,
in woodcuts and watermarks, sifting the stars down

through a gauze of glyph and scribble: one,
in tufted sleeves, rousing the Roundhead guards,

gibbering auguries; and another, divining
defeats, compassing silently under the spilled light

of a Cavalier moon. But it's a third my mind pinches
to conjure – his frowsed beard spinning

operas of rhombi, agonies of sphere.
Plucking the teeth of his astrolabe, he feels it –

the future splitting into slides: first a plague,
a fever, then a great fire. He blinks, and now

it's a darkening fleet, a factory's brick throat,
air-pumps dissecting breath, and, nearer now,

acid furring a birdless sky; an arid clenching of leaves,
the groan of oceans bulging. And there,

in the final frame, something more precise:
hands trembling in a library; an almanac

falling from my view; life's unfathomable
constellations fizzling out.

A Treatise Concerning the Perception of Ghosts

The rôle of eyes in seeing's hard to see –
how Matter came to Mind or which came first;
what once seemed real now look like ghosts to me.

Though mystics and astronomers agree,
the universe began with one great burst,
the rôle of eyes in seeing's hard to see.

Yet visionary life is far from free,
the flashes come or don't and years are lost;
what once seemed real now look like ghosts to me.

Take Berkeley, who unpicked Locke mentally,
unweaving angles where no lines are crossed:
the rôle of eyes in seeing's hard to see.

Or Plato, with his talk of trees and Tree –
of mists not merely mist but soul of frost;
what once seemed real now look like ghosts to me.

And then I reach for you, half-consciously,
forgetting what is gone must not be touched.
The rôle of eyes in seeing's hard to see;
what once seemed real now look like ghosts to me.

Puddles

What is it with toddlers and puddles? –
the half-inch of stagnant sky

that draws them in
                    to the shallow

of pavements, the slump
of gravel paths,

               bending low
to tap their reflections

with the dragged end of sticks, divining
themselves from beneath

the wobbling surface, coaxing
cowlicks and curls,

                   to find their eyes
slipping into the skim

of a long-legged fly, the dark scud
of clouds behind them –

clouds that will soon merge
puddle into puddle,

                  year into year,
until the whole world

is upside down.

The Lantern Cage

It is, I suppose, that old cliché
of not knowing

                    one was poor,
of making do

with what we had: toys
from shadows,

                    tales hanging
in the curtainless windows. And hunger

was a thing left
undefined. After carving

the bluetit, we would pluck it
clean of meat

                    for sandwiches,
boil the breast's brittle

                              lantern cage
for stock and after a few days,

once the gristle dried, build
a bone machine

                    from the delicate
wreckage, we'd take turns

flying around the kitchen in,
after dark, after

                    the slippered slackskins
gone *nigh-nigh*.

Singlings

I can still see him through a gap
in the corrugation,

                               measure him
mashing the wort:

a pocked drum of barley and yeast
he'll wrist to a sap,

crocking it above peat in the cramp
of a mooned shed;

                               can still size him
sieving a flask of singlings

to souse the blackleg calves with,
balm his daughter's swell,

                               cure the village
rash – *impetigo, gout, The King's Evil*

and *The Viper's Dance*; can still sync
my mind to the dark

                               eloquence
of his awkward alchemy, coaxing spirit

from a wormed tun – turf vowels,
trough blood –

                               churning the earth
to a fire of tears.

The Lemures

For three nights the temples shut –
no marriage vows exchanged.
For three nights, fists of beans

opened like rain across the graves, skins
smouldered in ceramic boats
while empty kettles rang with the sharp

knuckle of a bone. This was bad enough.
And whether or not it succeeded
in keeping away the evil spirits

of the evil dead was pointless
to debate. For three nights each year,
at least we had a plan.

On Missing the Cherry Blossoms

They were just on the verge of blooming
　　when you went away to Spain –
their knowledge of something coming,
　　undecrypted by the rain.

They were just on the cusp of cracking,
　　and divulging all they knew,
but you were away, not looking,
　　and I was looking for you.

Irish Fish

'Whatever you do,' I said, waiting for the line
to twitch, 'don't give in to the lazy list poem,
those rigmaroles of insects and flowers, ice creams
and clouds', when suddenly, a pound of slippery light

flashed to the surface, its ambiguous scales
tipping the balance against me: a whipsnout sorcerer
or an arctic telescope, a velvet belly lantern shark
or a thorny skate, a knifetooth dogfish or an undulate

ray, a narrownose chimera or a fivebeard rockling,
a smalleyed rabbitfish or a glasshead grenadier,
a bulbous dreamer or an arrowtooth eel, a nine-
spined stickleback or a viviparous blenny, a goldsinny

wrasse or a shorthorn sculpin, a rakery beaconlamp
or a diaphanous hatchet… 'Stop!' I said,
catching myself, 'a diaphanous hatchet? C'mon
man, you're just making this stuff up.'

Table Saw

for my father

I must have watched a thousand times
the high whinging whirr

of spun steel squeal into the split
skin of measured ply, oak, or cherry,

studying the feel, the firm
finesse his steady shoulder would

impress upon each supplicating plank –
the way a poet separates from prose

syllable and sound, emptiness from ink –
lost in a must of sweet sawdust,

never seeing how the pieces dove
together, that days and weeks can't build

forever, but shapes strange, invisible
as ether; how much of how I'm cut

comes down through him: this
misangled joint, that crooked limb.

Be Right Back

If anyone calls, I'll be down
by the edge

                skimming stones,
scrabbling in the tide,

contemplating how
with every pulse

                of wristed slate,
some part of me

disperses, walks on water, skitters
along a well-worn line

                  of setting suns.
If they come for me,

tell them I've stepped out,
a little shaky at first,

to find my feet gathering pace
above shelves

            of wave,
followed by another

and still another echo
of my flicked

              and sinking self.
Tell them that by now,

I'll have a good head start,
that anyone who wants

to get his hands on me
will need to know

                 what to feel for
(thin and flat and snug)

among the curling wash of shell
and brine,

          how to snap
the shoulder and slip the thumb,

to leave no sea or moon
or star unturned:

              to just let go.